# Ghost Hunting

## David Orme

## Contents

# Have you seen...

- strange lights that move?
- people that suddenly vanish?
- things that move by themselves?

# Have you heard...

- bumps in the night?
- footsteps when there's no one there?
- voices when there's no one there?
- the sound of screams, or rattling chains?

# Have you felt...

- suddenly cold when it is hot all around you?
- scared for no reason?

Could it be a ghost? Or could it be something ordinary?

This book will help you to decide!

# What is a ghost?

Ghosts might be:

- spirits of dead people that have become 'stuck' where they used to live, or where something terrible happened to them

- pictures from the past that some people are able to see – we do not know how this works. Some scientists think it might be to do with electrical changes in the air around us

- strange pictures, sounds and feelings made in our own brains – especially when we are scared or upset.

Many people were executed at the Tower of London. It is a famous place for ghosts!

# Why do we hear strange noises in the night?

Is it ghosts? Is it:

• animals?

Many creatures, such as bats and mice, are out at night.

The **death-watch beetle** makes a tapping noise by banging its head on timber.

- changes in temperature?

When it gets colder at night, some things shrink.
This can make floorboards and heating pipes
creak.

- the wind?

The wind can make strange noises when it blows
through windows, doors, and holes in the wall.

# Why do we see strange figures?

They may be ghosts … but they may not!

Our brains can sometimes make us see things that aren't really there. Our brain likes to make faces out of things. Can you see a face in this picture of the planet Mars?

Now look at the close up. Is it really a face?

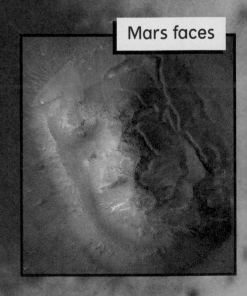

Mars faces

This photograph was taken at a World War II **gun emplacement** in Dover, Kent.

Can you see a strange figure in the circle?

Is it the mist? A real person? A ghostly soldier?

# What do you think?

# Can ghosts move things?

If things move by themselves, people say there is a **poltergeist** in the house.

This is a picture of Borley rectory, the most haunted house in England.

Strange things happened even after it burnt down. Can you see the brick floating in the air?

Poltergeists can:
- throw things around a room
- light fires
- tip you out of bed!

Many people have seen or heard such things. What could make them happen?

Is it:
- wicked spirits?
- spirits that like playing jokes?
- tricks played by living people?

# Investigating ghosts 1:
## Making reports

If someone says they have seen a ghost, you should:
- **interview** them as soon as you can
- ask them to tell their story

Do not interrupt them, but make careful notes.

- Write down:
  - what happened
  - when and where it happened
  - how well they could hear and see
  - names of any other people who were there

- Ask questions when they have told their story.

Use all the information to write a report.

# *Harlow*
# *Ghost-Hunters*
## *Club*

---

## *Witness questionnaire*

Date: ........................................................

Place: ........................................................

Weather: ........................................................

Name of witness: ........................................................

Address: ........................................................

Witness's statement: ........................................................

........................................................

........................................................

........................................................

........................................................

# Investigating ghosts 2:
## Studying history

If you think a house is haunted, try and find out about its history.

You could use:
- your local library
- the Internet

Questions to ask:
- Who has lived in the house?
- Has anything strange ever happened there?
- What was there before the house was built?

In York there is an old building called the Treasurer's House. People have seen ghosts of Roman soldiers marching through the cellar.

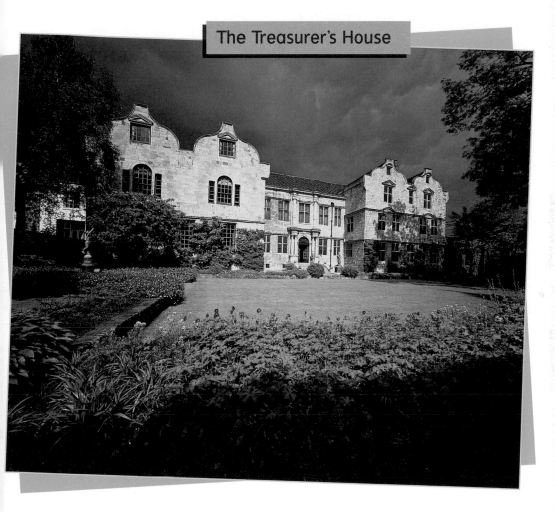

The Treasurer's House

**Historians** have found out that there used to be a Roman road in the same place!

# Investigating ghosts 3:
## Taking measurements

**Investigators** use special equipment.

- They use thermometers to measure temperature.

A **maximum/minimum thermometer** can record temperatures over a period of time.

An electronic thermometer is very accurate. It can show any cold spots in a room.

- They use meters to measure electrical changes.

Some scientists think that ghosts are caused by these changes in and around buildings.

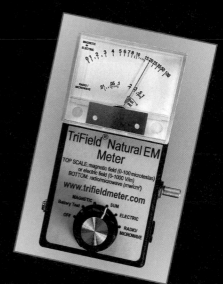

- They use a candle flame.

Candle flames help to see moving air or draughts.

# Investigating ghosts 4:
## Recording pictures and sounds

Investigators use special cameras. These can be left in haunted places. They take a photograph **automatically** if:

- a sound is made
- the temperature changes
- something moves.

Infrared imagery

Some cameras work in the dark.
They use **infra-red photography**.

**Video cameras** can be used to take
moving pictures.

**Microphones** can be set up to record
any sounds on tape or disk.

# Investigating ghosts 5:
## Fake ghosts

Can you see a ghost? Don't be fooled! This is a fake picture!

20

How was it made?

1. A 'ghost' was drawn with white crayon on clear plastic.

2. This was put onto a picture of a dark room.

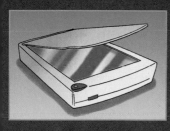

3. The picture was scanned into a computer.

Sometimes people pretend their houses are haunted. Why?

- to make themselves famous
- to sell their story for money
- because they like playing jokes
- to attract visitors!

Ghost hunters have to be careful not to be fooled!

Ye Olde Haunted Inn

# Are there such things as ghosts?

Evidence FOR ghosts:

- Many people say they have seen them.
- Sometimes more than one person has seen the same ghost at different times
- Photographs have been taken showing ghosts.

Real or fake?

22

Evidence AGAINST ghosts:

- Ghosts and ghost photographs are easy to fake.
  It is very easy to fool people!
- Ghosts do not fit in with what we know about science.
- No one has ever proved that ghosts exist.

So … are there such things as ghosts?

# What do you think?

# Glossary

**automatically**  working by itself, does not need a person to operate it

**death-watch beetle**  a beetle found in damp wood

**gun emplacement**  place where a large gun was positioned

**historian**  a person who studies history

**infra-red photography**  a type of photography that shows where there is heat, not light

**interview**  when you talk to a person and write down what they tell you

**investigator**  a person who tries to find the truth about something that has happened

**maximum/minimum thermometer**  a special thermometer that records the hottest and coldest temperatures over a period of time

**microphone**  something which picks up sound so that it can be recorded

**poltergeist**  when objects move all by themselves, people say it is caused by a poltergeist

**video camera**  a camera to record moving pictures